THE EASTER STORY

Retold by Sophie Piper
Illustrated by Annabel Spenceley

LION
CHILDREN'S

Clip clop, clip clop. The donkey's hooves clattered on the road. The noise made people turn.

"Look who's coming!" said someone. "It's Jesus, and he's riding to Jerusalem for the festival."

"He's told us how to be part of God's kingdom," said another. "Perhaps he's going to make it all happen, and declare himself king!"

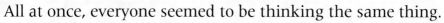

All at once, everyone seemed to be thinking the same thing.

"Here comes the king," they shouted.

"Hooray for the king!"

They cut palm branches and waved them.

They laid their cloaks on the ground to carpet the way.

Surely, *surely*, they thought, Jesus is about to do something that will turn the world upside down.

Once in Jerusalem, Jesus did do something spectacular.
   He went to the Temple, where there was a festival market.
   "This is not a place for buying and selling," cried Jesus.
His voice was angry.
   "It's meant to be the place to say prayers to God."
He chased all the market people away.

Tut tut tut. The priests and the teachers were not just annoyed – they were furious.

"Jesus is a troublemaker," they agreed.

"People think his teaching is good and wise. They like the words about 'God's love' and 'God's forgiveness'.

"How dare he say he knows all about God!

"How dare he upset everything in the Temple.

"We're going to get rid of him."

While some of Jesus' best friends got ready for a festival meal, one of them did something very cruel.

That one was Judas Iscariot. He went to Jesus' enemies. "I'll help you catch him," he said. "If you pay me."

s friends went to a garden of olive trees,
ould sleep that night.
kness, Judas came back. With him
s. They grabbed Jesus and
n off to his enemies.

At the festival meal, Jesus shared the bread and wine.
  "When I am gone, I want you to share a meal like this,"
he said. "It will be the way to remember me.
          "And there's something else you must do:
          love one another.

"That will show everyone that you
Eleven good friends listened.
The one named Judas Iscariot slipp

Jesus and h
where they
  In the da
were soldie
marched h

At the festival meal, Jesus shared the bread and wine.
   "When I am gone, I want you to share a meal like this,"
he said. "It will be the way to remember me.
                     "And there's something else you must do:
                     love one another.

"That will show everyone that you are truly my followers."
Eleven good friends listened.
The one named Judas Iscariot slipped away.

Jesus and his friends went to a garden of olive trees, where they could sleep that night.

In the darkness, Judas came back. With him were soldiers. They grabbed Jesus and marched him off to his enemies.

"You're a troublemaker!" they told Jesus. "We'll have you punished for all you've done."

They took him to the man who was in charge of all the punishments, Pontius Pilate.

That very day, a Friday, they arranged for Jesus to be put to death on a cross.

Jesus didn't fight back. He even said a prayer for his enemies.

"Father God, forgive them. They don't understand what they are doing."

Slowly, sorrowfully, Jesus died. Friends came and laid him in a tomb. They rolled the stone door shut.

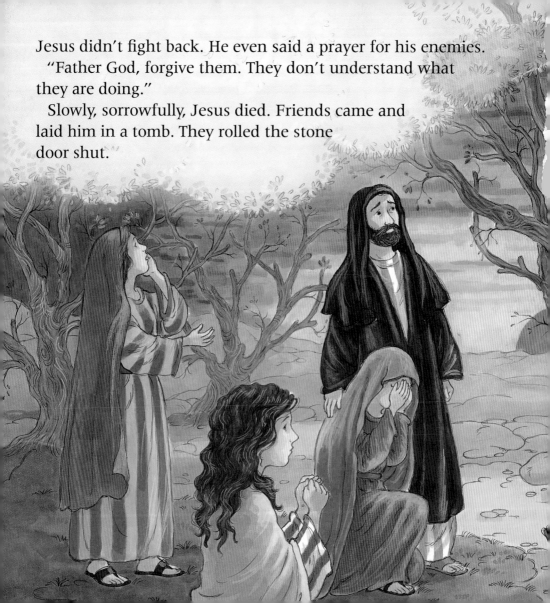

The sabbath day of rest came and went.

Early on Sunday morning, some women came
back to the tomb, to say a last goodbye to their
friend Jesus.

What they saw made them dismayed and astonished.

The tomb was open.

The body was gone.

An angel spoke to them.

"Jesus is not here. God has given him new life."

In the hours and days that followed, Jesus appeared to his friends and disciples. It was hard to believe, but they really could see him and touch him. The angel's message was true.

Jesus spent time talking to them. "Soon I will go to my father God in heaven," he said.

"I will make everything ready to welcome those who obey my words: those who love one another and forgive one another.

"Go and tell everyone in the whole wide world this good news:
"God loves you, and welcomes you into his kingdom."

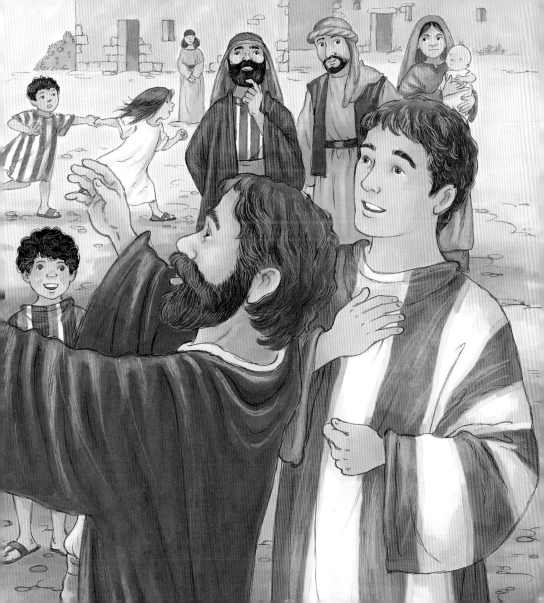